FIT FOR TH

GOLF

TED POLLARD

WARD LOCK

Text © Ted Pollard
© Ward Lock Limited 1991

Writer: John Ingham
Editor: Heather Thomas
Art director: Rolando Ugolini

Text set in Univers Medium by Ipswich Typographics Ltd
Printed and bound in Great Britain by Richard Clay Ltd, Bungay Suffolk

**British Library Cataloguing in Publication
Data**

Pollard, Ted
  Golf.
  1. Sports. Health
  I. Title II. Series
  613.711

ISBN 0-7063-6932-7

Ted Pollard

If you want a better swing, the golf professional can help. If you want a better body to ensure a better swing, then the gym can fix it. So combine the two skills, and you have Ted Pollard, karate expert who doubled for Bruce Lee on stage, one-time wrestler and a man who can hold centre stage. What Ted has to say makes original and compelling reading for the golfer — amateur or professional.

Ted was born in Barbados and the first sport he ever played was table-tennis at the YMCA in Bridgetown. From there he took an interest in body-building in order to develop his maximum physical potential.

What follows in Ted's life is a story in itself. Ted quickly took up and excelled in the sports that appealed to him — boxing, roller-skating and cycling — and achieved astonishing results. Little wonder, then, that when he discovered golf, by accident, he developed a special system that enabled him to play rounds with scores in the 70's within two years.

This book, therefore, is a totally original approach to achieving a high level of golf fitness and thereby playing better golf and makes compulsory reading for professionals and weekend players alike.

Acknowledgments

The author and publishers wish to thank the following who kindly helped in the production of this book: Apollo Golf Shafts, the Ben Hogan Equipment Company, the Cobra Golf Club Company, the Dunlop Company, the Polysport Company, Yasuo (Randy) Doi of Matsushita Electric Works Ltd, and photographers Mark Shearman, Ian Brand and Phil Inglis together with professionals Hugh Boyle and Simon Buckley. Also: Surrey, England, golfing twins Jo and Samantha Head as well as Robert A. de Stolfe, theatrical photographer of Miami, Florida. This book was written in collaboration with British golf writer John Ingham.

Dedication

I wish to extend my grateful appreciation to the Baron and Baroness Von Pantz whose assistance and support have made my golf, and this book, possible.

Photographs
All the photographs in this book were
taken by Mark Shearman with the exception
of the following:
Ben Hogan company: page 72
Ian Brand: pages 76-78
Sir Henry Cotton: pages 28,29
Peter Dazeley: pages 52-53
Alfred Dunhill Ltd: page 59
Dunlop Company: Page 75
Phil Inglis: pages 6, 41, 75
Robert A. de Stolfe: page 9

CONTENTS

FOREWORD
by Bernard Gallacher
1991 Ryder Cup Captain

I have worked with Ted Pollard in Europe and feel that his ideas to develop golf from an athletic point of view are excellent.

In the past, some of the great champions didn't reach their ultimate potential because they had not developed their swing muscles with specialized training of any kind, or exercises remotely similar to those outlined by Ted in this book.

Look at the recent champions whose careers were filled with pain and you will see that the list is an impressive one. Back troubles have afflicted Seve Ballesteros, Lee Trevino and even Jack Nicklaus.

The modern golfer today is an athlete and it was Gary Player who blazed the keep-fit trail. In fact, Gary went further; he said you should first get fit, and then become even fitter, and allied good diet with a physical training campaign that might have overwhelmed a less determined individual.

Interestingly, Ted says even Gary Player would have been a greater champion if he had included a flexibility programme based around his golf swing. Such a fitness programme, says Ted, would have helped Gary to keep his shape and posture over the years.

Ted tells us that golf is not an unnatural game, provided that you are flexible. He says strain on the spine is caused because the body cheats in order to bring the clubhead into the ball in a square position. He outlines why a true athlete can make a full and correct swing at the golf ball without ever lifting the left heel and he tells us, and shows us, exercises to counter the frequent faults caused by incorrect positions.

The late Sir Henry Cotton used to say that you cannot be too strong for golf and Gary Player certainly agreed with this. Top golfer Nick Faldo has cycled and jogged thousands of miles and is a fine example of the modern athletic golfer. This book comes as a breath of fresh air, and brings a whole new approach to golf. Are we fit for golf? In most cases, says Ted Pollard, the answer is ''No'' — but at least he doesn't leave us stranded; he shows us the way to more powerful and consistent play.

Ted Pollard shows Ryder Cup captain Bernard Gallacher that trunk rotation is vital in good golf.

INTRODUCTION

Almost everyone I meet wants to play better golf. By reading this book you could be taking the first step to becoming more powerful and the only question you need ask is: "How badly do I want to improve?" I hope the answer is along the lines that you really do want to become a more powerful hitter of the ball, and that you will give my advice and coaching your best shot.

Nobody is a born athlete. I made myself strong, learned karate and the art of balance, and quickly became a low-handicap golfer. Although I am no longer a young man, I have the flexibility of youth and try to combine this with the agility of a gymnast.

Believe me, a clear eye and toned muscles can transform your game — and it will over the coming weeks. Even oldish muscle can be trained to make a better and wider swing at the ball. I see many club players who are out of condition, and even some professionals on the Tour. Their muscle is not unlike an elastic band that has been kept in a refrigerator. They hurry to the first tee with their chilled muscle, make a pass at the ball, and often do themselves serious damage which, although maybe not noticed for an hour or so, causes them to seize up on the inward nine holes, rather like a car engine that seizes up through lack of oil.

My theories are simple: I want to put the oil into your golf swing. I intend to describe two-sided training. On the backswing, I stress trunk flexibility and on the forward swing, I will demonstrate just how important are the left shoulder muscles in pulling the clubhead into a powerful hitting position. Only then will you use the guiding right side

and hand to deliver the hit.

Karate and golf have much in common. If I want a controlled blow at an opponent in karate, I must set myself up correctly, and in perfect balance, to deliver that blow with the maximum impact. In boxing they sometimes talk about hitting their weight. In golf many players never hit their weight and are unable to get into a position to do so. In fact most golfers merely fan the ball. My instruction will enable you to smash it down the fairway with much more power and control.

This brings me back to you. How passionate and committed are you to improve your golf and to get fitter? Will you commit yourself to these goals? I assume you will and now intend to guide you.

Flexibility

Correct flexibility training is overlooked by the majority of athletes, particularly in golf. Very few young professionals understand the fundamental importance of flexibility training and some will actually tell you that golf is not an athletic pursuit. However, modern golf is just that.

As you know, when young, the body recovers quickly from minor injuries. It does not seem logical to spend a few minutes warming up before practice, or play. However, I'm sure there are many top players today who wish they had devoted a small part of their preparation to correct training, based around their particular swing.

I believe that all aspiring golfers should

take a body-building course. I am not suggesting Mr Universe-type preparation, nor am I advocating that you lift heavy weights. My body-building programme is purely to learn and understand how your arms and legs work, how the number of 'repetitions' or push-ups affects the endurance and the development of specific muscle groups.

My training will help you understand how the body works during the swing. Muscle endurance and flexibility go hand in hand; one depends on the other and vice versa. If the teacher of golf only understands the swing, he is at a disadvantage. Some coaches attempt to inflict on a pupil a method that the pupil may not physically be able to carry out on the course. Every human being is different and an untrained body cannot hit the ball like a youthful Gary Player, no matter how hard that golfer tries.

It is true that the golf swing has been taught with some success over the past years. However, you will agree that most of

This position, in karate terms, represents the top of a backswing. Now I'm resisting the urge to hit and, finally (right) at the 11th hour, I deliver a maximum blow — and the belt position is a key factor in hip movement, for karate and golf. What I'm saying is: you can utilize karate methods to boost your golf.

the modern stars learned the game at a young age, interestingly before they had reached adulthood and they were capable of using fully developed bodies — to hit. Therefore the only way youngsters learned to play properly was to develop balance and timing, and a good swing was the almost automatic result. Young golfers know that the only way to send the ball a long way is to swing through the ball.

However, older golfers learning this game, face a serious handicap. They try to hit hard at the ball with strong hands and grown-up muscle and their attempt to crunch shots out of sight means the right shoulder goes over the top, and so does their game.

So a teacher who understands swing techniques will usually suceed with the young pupil. Once the teacher gives the correct swing 'key', the young muscle will develop and all that is needed is dedication.

On the other hand, if that same youngster was to take up golf in his mid-thirties, the same teacher might not have similar success, and the reason has nothing to do with age. The truth is that the major muscle groups such as the deltoids in the shoulders and the trapeziuses (the muscles that run across the back of the neck and shoulders) are fully developed and this creates the urge to hit from the top of the backswing, rather than swinging down into, and through, the shot as youngsters do.

When the body is fully developed the teacher who understands only the golf swing and not the body mechanics, is at a great disadvantage. But if strength and flexibility exist through correct training, then great success can be achieved by a pupil prepared to work.

When I first started training in Marbella, Spain, my question to a local professional was: "Can you explain how the body works and which muscle groups I should use?" I received no intelligent answer, and I never do, either in Europe or the United States.

Without doubt, flexibility forms the foundation of the golf swing. Inflexibility means a golfer will always sustain a series of niggling injuries throughout his golfing life.

The main areas usually affected are:
- Neck and trapezius area, being the muscles that run across the back of the neck and shoulders. The problem usually lies on the right side — the opposite side, obviously, for left-handed players.

- Shoulder joints which lack flexibility and rotation.
- Wrists which lack strength and flexibility.
- Back problems, also associated with lack of flexibility, bad posture and a poor finish position.
- Elbow pain which is caused by swing faults.

The idea of devoting some time to better preparation is that it will enable you to enjoy your golf, and it will ensure that you get the opportunity to improve. This positive attitude will mean that rather than waiting to see if your game is suddenly thrown into reverse because of an injury, you will be able to look ahead, and forward, to more powerful play.

I want you to study the photographs throughout this book, together with the captions, and fully understand them. Don't rush at it, and remember to devote some time, every day, to becoming a better golfer. After all, it is a game that you can play and enjoy all your life, and that doesn't mean a lifetime of pain!

In this book I present the specialist programme I developed to deal specifically with the game of golf. The advice was acquired from developing training programmes for countless amateurs, both in Europe and the United States. In addition sixty European touring profesionals at the annual Apollo week have benefited during the Volvo Tour Training School.

My programme requires some discipline and dedication from each pupil, but it is relevant to the touring professional as well as the teenage scratch player and the 60-year-old high handicapper. I know my training methods work and represent a solid foundation on which to base your game.

CHAPTER ONE

LET'S GET STARTED

The fundamental importance of correct training

Having worked, and worked-out, at clubs world-wide, including two leading health clubs in London, I have always looked around during my training sessions and watched the way other people tackle training. I see the same mistakes being made in the gym as you can see on the golf driving ranges or practice pitches. People with good intentions are simply going about it in the wrong way.

I believe all serious effort, in any field of activity, should be rewarded and I intend to guide you to good results with a structured exercise programme and a grading system aimed at the beginner, the young semi-athlete, and the player who merely needs to be shown the way to even better and more powerful golf.

I don't expect you to complete the entire programme at every session, nor do I want you to exhaust yourself. My advice is to go through each exercise several times, and to make sure you enjoy it. My aim is to isolate each movement best suited to your needs.

How? Well, from the Address Position in golf, to the position I call the 'Half Backswing', I recommend trunk twists, and also golf bag twists. Both these exercises are explained and both aim at making the trunk of your body more flexible.

The bag twist encourages you to turn your trunk against the hips on the backswing, absolutely essential if you wish your body to create a platform from which to deliver a powerful hit. Believe me, this is one of the secrets of good golf.

Exercise allied to my programmed training is not just for your golf. It will improve your general level of fitness and sense of well-being because you will feel better and more inclined to tackle any sport with extra confidence.

Modern golf is now a whole new ball game. Competitors who used to 'train' at the 19th hole and did not care about being overweight and out of condition, no longer win the big prizes. Athletes are now giving the winning speeches.

I have worked at my total fitness for years and excelled in many sports, and I quickly discovered when I turned to golf, that there is a strong similarity between swinging a golf club powerfully, and delivering a serious blow, with maximum impact, in karate. Think about the terrific impact speed of a clubhead, driven by a player like Ian Woosnam, and you can see that fitness, excellent co-ordination and correct teaching, are essential. Good golf is not a gift: it has to be worked for, and worked at.

Obviously it is more satisfying to teach youngsters about fitness because they will far more readily reach a high standard. The twins featured in some of the photographs look fit, but even they could improve their strength, flexibility and hitting ability. Few of the top American women professionals look muscular and unattractive, yet many devote much of their time to keeping fit.

To be successful at golf, you must maximize your fitness. A parent aged 60 will not achieve the same muscle tone and bounce in the legs as will a son or daughter. But all of us who are not so young can reduce our scores, and maybe our waist-lines, with a sensible attitude.

I should like to see club professionals on the first tee every Sunday morning, not only watching particularly young club members, but also offering advice to each based on their individual needs. This would not only show that the club professional cares that his pupils enjoy a better performance, but it would also emphasise that golf is a continual game of improvement. Nobody ever fully learned the game and even top champions like Jack Nicklaus and Arnold Palmer still tinker with their golf. In fact, as Palmer's hair became greyer, many observers noticed that his swing and balance improved. He had to swing the club more smoothly and his slashing, attacking golf that we all enjoyed years ago gave way to a smoother swing. Nicklaus, in fact, claimed he had never hit the ball as far, or as well, as when he won the US Masters as an 'old' man in 1986.

So my advice will always be to get fitter than ever and insist that your local professional looks your game over. He will probably be pleased that you are persisting, and your improvement will be a good advertisement for him.

Rest periods

It is important to time each rest period between exercises. The secret is not to rush from one exercise to another, but conversely not to allow yourself too lengthy a rest. I allow myself around 30-40 seconds between easy drills and exercises. If, however, the exercise is tough, then I extend my rest period. The endurance of each individual differs and you are the best judge of your own rest periods.

People who train seriously find that their bodies automatically tell them when to rest, and when to resume exercising. Good sense must prevail.

Programme of golf drills and exercises

Beginner's programme	Sets	Repetitions
Side bends	1	8-10
Overhead shoulder stretch	1	8-10
Seated knees to chest, with forward-stretch	1	8-10
Alternate knees-to-chest (lying down)	1	8-10
Standing alternate knees-to-chest	1	8-10
Seated two-way stretch	1	8-10
Roll up to toes	1	8-10
Cat stretch	1	8-10
Lying half-twists	1	8-10
Standing tall drill	1	8-10
Half-twist	1	8-10

The programme shown here is structured for beginners. Those more advanced should increase the number of sets to two and the repetitions should increase to between 10 and 15 per exercise. For the highly skilled, I recommend a further increase, depending on the discomfort the exercise has caused. However, on no account should any student over-train on any given session.

Training explanation: a set is one specific exercise that is repeated for a specified number of times. Each exercise should be completed before moving on to the next one.

FIT FOR THE GAME: GOLF

Identical twins Jo and Samantha Head from Goodwood Golf Club, Surrey, show the way with a side-bend sequence which assists shoulder and trunk flexibility.

Side bends

1 Stand with feet apart and arms at the sides, erect and relaxed.

2 Each girl is showing perfect extension with a vertically upstretched arm.

3 They are stretching vital golfing muscles as they bend sideways.

The most important feature of this exercise is not to collapse the outstretched arm at any time. Believe me, this isn't as easy as it looks. Repeat the exercise the opposite way. Start with 8-10 repetitions.

Good golf comes from a flexible body, and the American star Fred Couples and Spaniard Seve Ballesteros are good examples of this, although recently Seve seems to have tightened up in his shoulder area. However, there is a cure for tight shoulders. Opposite the Head twins and I are performing the daily routine I recommend to every golfer, young or old. Flexible shoulders eliminate what experts call the 'flying' elbow. The aim is to attain maximum flexibility. To achieve this, my pupils must break down shoulder stiffness, often caused by inactivity.

Overhead shoulder stretch

Body joints can become 'fused' or stiff through lack of use. In older people we talk about breaking down the adhesions and sometimes you can never release rusted-up joints. However, having a positive attitude and doing daily exercises will help everyone acquire a freer swing which will produce extra yards. So here's what you do:

2

1 Stand with your feet shoulder width apart, interlock both thumbs, extending the fingers fully and stretching the arms above your head.
2 You can make it tougher by stretching even further. You can see that one of the girls (left) is more flexible than the other — and it shows in her back arch which means she's cheated slightly on the intended exercise. The ideal position is mine (centre).

Why lie down to exercise?

You may wonder why I am on the ground, doing exercises like this. I am building strong mid-section muscles which come into play when any golfer makes a backswing, or comes sweeping into the ball for a powerful hit. Other benefits of this trunk rotation include shoulder flexibility — essential co-ordination because hand and leg movements are being trained to act as one.

Alternate knees to chest

1 Lie down flat on your back with your legs fully stretched and your hands placed, with finger tips touching, behind your head. Now raise your head and ensure that your back is as flat as possible on the ground. Follow this fully to work on the right muscles.

2 The exercise starts with the right foot still grounded while the left leg is raised and bent with the knee touching the right elbow. My right shoulder has come up to meet it while my trunk has rotated slightly. This is developing golfing muscles and slimming your mid section at the same time.

3 And finally this is where the whole body takes the strain. Top coaches do not always realise that this exercise assists in developing definition of the thigh muscles which contribute to the foundation of the whole golf swing. Notice that as the right knee meets the left elbow, the exercise is now in full flow and both legs remain airborne.

> **Caution: At no time should the head touch the ground because if this is allowed, the back will be obliged to take the strain, and our intention is to promote abdominal development.**
>
> **Remember that this whole motion is one continuous movement. Start off with 8 repetitions and gradually build up to 15 as you get stronger and more flexible.**

1

2

3

You too can have elastic muscles

The backs of the legs need stretching, no matter how fit you are. This exercise is the perfect way to warm-up the abdominal muscles and acts as an excellent routine for building flexibility in the backs of the legs — something essential for almost any sport.

Seated knees-to-chest

1 Sit on the ground with legs outstretched and palms of the hands on the ground.

2 With your arms outstretched to the sides, slowly lean forwards, stretching out over your legs.

3 Grab your ankles with your hands.

4 If you are as flexible as me, you can clasp your heels in your hands and stretch down until your head is resting on your knees.

5 Slowly unwind out of the stretch to your original position and raise your legs off the ground, with knees bent. Repeat 8 times.

4

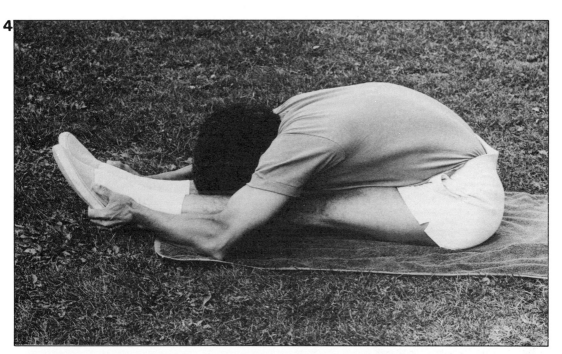

5

The dreaded seated two-way stretch

Although this may look impossible, you will find that after two or three weeks of persevering, the extended movement shown here will make you looser, and more flexible.

The first few times that you try this exercise, you may feel some aches and pains afterwards but this is quite natural and will decrease, over the weeks. As with all exercise, a little a day will benefit you more than rushing at it like so many people do in health clubs and gyms.

Seated two-way stretch (below)

Extend the legs and it is possible that *your* legs will not be splayed out so wide as mine. At all times, however, the body position must follow faithfully what you see in regard to foot alignment with the knees. Likewise the back, at all times, must be erect, as though you plan to put your stomach on the ground and not your head nor the chest which would cause an arching of the back. Realise that this is an exercise in itself, and that your hands are acting as a support as you go from upright to a forward 'rock'. Lean gently forward and place your palms flat on the ground in front of you, hands facing inwards. Gently raise your body to an erect position. Repeat 8 times.

The dreaded three-way stretch

1 By criss-crossing my hands in this side-stretch I'm controlling my foot and leg to prevent them splaying over to the right. When that happens you're cheating, to ease the tension. Notice that at no time are my knees lifted off the ground, despite the urge to do so. Stretch to the right and then raise your body slowly back to the original position.

2 Now, stretching to the left, my back has not collapsed and I'm stretching towards my left foot, with my eye on my toe. Head, knee and toe are in perfect alignment. I'm doing this to ensure that I benefit from the fullest possible stretch. My friends joke that I'm putting people on the rack, and they're not far wrong!

3 The final picture of me with my chest and

stomach touching my thigh is really advanced flexibility and something that takes time and practice to achieve. Nevertheless, as you get increasingly supple and flexible, you can strive to achieve this.

Depending on your own mobility, you should work within the boundaries possible for you. Do not over-stretch beyond the limits of your body. Do 8-10 repetitions of this exercise.

Caution: Like the profesionals who start their practice routine with easy 9-iron shots, and then move towards their driver, you, too, should ease yourself gradually into this exercise. Contrary to public opinion, exercise should not hurt. Train, don't strain.

There's more to this than meets the eye . . .

. . . so we reach for the sky!
Here are five movements that will make you better at any sport you play. They stretch almost every part of an athlete's body and help develop good balance, which is essential for controlled hitting at golf.

Standing tall drill

1 A flagpole is the straightest thing on a golf course and I want you to attempt the almost impossible. A straight body is an athletic body and means total control: vital for every part of the swing. For this movement, interlock your hands by curling one thumb round the other. Stand comfortably — and reach for the sky!

2 Stretch forward into a reverse 'L' shape. You must have a perfectly straight back to ensure that your leg muscles are at full s-t-r-e-t-c-h. Keep your feet flat on the ground. My back is flat to avoid injury while the back of my legs take the strain.

3 And now, we're into what I call the cat stretch. Don't be put off but this little exercise will develop both strength and body-flex at the back which prevent those injuries that occur almost every week on the golf course. I'm arching my back deliberately to create flexibility in the back which, if achieved, will help protect the most aggressive golfer. Note the position of my hands with the fingers resting on my thighs just above the knees.

4 I'm slowly straightening my body as I move my hands upwards, past my stomach and up towards my chest. You'll see that my chin is buried almost into my neck.

5 This looks a bit like the opening picture, but I'm on my toes and my hands have rejoined and, once again, I'm reaching for the sky, at maximum stretch. All these exercises

as you'll see in the Programme on page 12, have to be repeated. Start with 8 repetitions and build up slowly as you become more flexible.

> **Caution: Don't over-extend, particularly in picture 2. Go as far as possible, until you reach your own personal limit. You need to feel the stretch without actually putting yourself in pain.**

'Ouch' exercises

Roll up to toes

1 This, in a way, is a highly advanced follow-up to your previous exercise. Don't be discouraged if you can't even get halfway near this position but the benefit to you will come if you *try* on a regular basis to practise along these lines. First, on no account, should you arch your back to arrive in position one. Many top sports people can't even touch the ground and are afraid of trying to do so because of a dodgy back. They don't know how wrong they are because fear of back pain will prevent them from releasing those tightened up and taut muscles. Because of a perfectly straight back throughout the exercise, my hamstrings and not my back are forced to

take the strain. Stand with your feet shoulder width apart, heels on the ground. Keeping your legs straight, slowly lower your body until your palms rest flat on the ground in front of you. Hold the stretch.

2 This is merely an advanced form of the roll-up position of the cat stretch on page 27 and in this instance you will see that the hands are placed separately on each foot instep, and the back is arched. The full upward hand 'sweep' exercise can begin here for high-achievers. Other golfers can start in accordance with their bending capability and that, as we've said, is the key. Everyone's body is different and it is up to you not to go beyond your limits.

Balance in motion

Golf is flexibility, balance and control, and you have only to watch certain weekenders on the first tee, falling about, to realise how little understood this is. So what do we do?

I have never, ever, heard a professional asked to teach the vital business of good balance. So let me describe this simple-looking exercise which, in fact, although extremely difficult, is very worthwhile.

Standing alternate knees-to-chest

1 First stand with feet shoulder-width apart with your fingers interlocking gently behind your head.

2 Try to resemble a spiral staircase. This is achieved by half twisting the upper body on the backswing while the right leg and foot are moved in the opposite direction. So balancing on your left leg raise your right leg with knee bent towards the left. At the same time, turn your upper body towards the right. Finally, reverse the process by stepping on the other leg.

> **Caution: Don't dip your head and shoulders towards the ground as you perform the exercise.**
>
> **Without trunk flexibility and perfect balance, this exercise will prove daunting. You may lose your balance at first and topple over. But persevere, and your balance will improve, and so will your golf swing.**

The half-twist

This exercise stretches the muscles used in the golfing backswing and follow through. When you roll over towards the left, you stretch the backswing muscles, and when you roll towards the right you stretch the muscles used in the follow-through.

1 Begin with the correct preparation: keep the feet and knees together. The back must be pressed against the ground or floor, and the arms must be fully outstretched. Now the hard part: the head must always remain upright, as shown. Raise your feet off the ground with your knees bent and close together. Do 8-10 repetitions.

2 Holding your legs above the ground, roll over to the left. You want the thighs and knees to roll over towards the left while, at the same time, trying to keep the shoulders pinned to the ground. If the trunk is inflexible, the shoulders will want to follow the turn of the hips which, in golfing terms, resembles a collapsed position at the top of the backswing and believe me, many quite good weekenders suffer from this problem. Now reverse what we called the backswing stretch. Feet and knees together, as before, remain in the same curled-up position and roll over to the right. Once again, try to keep your shoulders on the ground, with the head erect.

> **Note: No caution is really required here because if the effort becomes too great, the shoulders will roll, according to the degree of twist.**

And now, into the animal kingdom of the cat stretch . . .

One of the most lithe animals in the world is the young kitten, the epitome of flexibility. We can learn from them by practising this exercise.

Cat stretch

1 Kneel with your knees and ankles touching. Your hands should be flat on the ground but not ahead of your shoulders. If they are, the exercise becomes less effective. Keep your eyes down and your back straight.

2 Try to roll your head down, almost towards your belt buckle while arching your back upwards. At no time should your arms collapse. Gently arch your back like a cat stretching.

3 Finally, arch in the opposite direction: head up, almost looking to the sky if possible. All this achieves back flexibility which, as we've said, is so important to defend yourself against everyday injuries. Do 8-10 repetitions to start off, and build up gradually to more.

CHAPTER TWO

FLEXIBILITY

I'm often asked this question: "Why should I spend time on developing body extension movements, or any other form of training, when I only play golf for fun?"

My answer is quite simple. As we age, the body's natural flexibility decreases and this leads to a greater risk of injury as golfers, not as young as they were, still try to turn on the backswing, and extend fully through the shot.

By giving some time to the exercise programme, not only will you play better golf and endure a less painful *aprés golf,* but you will also have the benefit of leading a fitter and healthier life. Winners are those who can complete a full trunk turn which puts their shoulders at approximately 90°. They can make a pass at the ball from this position without any discomfort. If you can achieve this, you too will start ahead of the game.

Many parts of the body can be trained through the golf swing, particularly the stomach muscles — and I'd like to explain how. First, seat yourself comfortably, holding a golf club behind your neck with both hands level with your shoulders. Now turn your trunk until your right shoulder is behind you, taking care not to dip the left shoulder. This rotation develops flexibility on the backswing, without over-rotating the hips, something that can wreck any golf shot. This exercise has the additional benefit of helping you slim the mid-section and build up stronger abdominal muscle.

This seated exercise is no secret; it has been used by millions all over the world but not often by golfers. The lack of knowledge about the correct movements and exercise for golf is something I intend to address here and, in certain cases, it is possible to keep in shape without training, if you know the technique. For instance, take the pre-swing exercise you sometimes see Nick Faldo and several other top players doing as they warm up. They place the club behind the neck (exactly as in the seated trunk exercise I will describe later). The slight difference is that the hips rotate and the left shoulder dips during the backswing twisting movement.

But, within the pages of this book, I will show you how best to keep your body in shape while training to improve your golf.

Given the right degree of flexibility, incorrect swing positions can be ironed out quickly. Once a pupil has achieved elasticity, co-ordination and timing are always close at hand. Combining the two helps to build the perfect foundation for tackling any swing change.

I continue to stress the importance of maximizing your stretching ability because without it your game will never come close to reaching its full potential. Each body has a different structure, and some are more loose than others. But that does not mean a less flexible person cannot be trained to develop a more fluid body.

The basic golf swing is carried out from the trunk. The swing is not an unusual movement if the body is correctly prepared to deal with rotating the trunk around the neck. Firstly, ignore the old saying: "Make a bigger shoulder turn". What we should concentrate on is trunk rotation. Without a full trunk twist, you can forget ever reaching that 90° turn with your shoulders. Trunk and neck flexibility are crucial. The only way you can complete the turn is with the movement of the hands, arms, shoulders, trunk and hips — there is no other effective way.

Jack Nicklaus and Arnold Palmer both played differently in their youth because they both enjoyed the luxury of flexibility, even though Nicklaus was fairly bulky. You should notice that neither have lifted their left heels and both have turned their trunks while retaining their hips in almost a square position to the target-line. The secret to this highly sprung coil position is not lost on certain superstars but requires maintenance. Many golfers overlook this aspect and cease to attain their youthful brilliance. In the case of both these fine players they adjusted their swings over the years to compensate for a body that no longer obliged in quite the same way.

Position generates power

We are looking at former Ryder Cup player Hugh Boyle in action as a senior player who is over fifty. But he still shoots scores well below 70. How does he do it? Although enjoying a fine swing, he might well have achieved even higher honours if he had trained with a programme based around his particular method.

The golf swing

1 Hugh's address position is excellent and shows that he is totally relaxed and in a position to make a sweeping movement away from the ball.

2 His half-backswing shows a slight over-rotation of the hips but the stress points are clearly shown in the hands, wrists, forearms and strong left-hand side shoulder muscles. The high right arm, at this point, is merely assisting in guiding. The main load-bearing limb is the left arm. Owing to his lack of trunk flexibility, the hips have been forced into an undesirable position too early in the backswing.

3 The top of the swing could be made even better if Hugh's trunk could turn against a more retaining hip position, similar to the younger Jack Nicklaus.

4 The secret to his brilliant game is the attacking angle shown vividly in this picture. The weight has been transferred on to his left side and, at the same time, his head remains as it was, at the address. Incidentally, you must note the retaining angle of the club. This is due to the splendid pulling action of the left hand, arm and side.

5 & 6 The final two pictures clearly show how Hugh's weight has been transferred onto the left side and his head and left foot are in almost perfect alignment: something that should ensure he will stay free of serious back problems.

Starting the swing

From address to halfway back

To walk on stage and then deliver a solid performance to a live audience is not an easy thing to do. And the more professional you become, the more difficult it is to start the ball rolling.

Golf, at the highest level, is like that. Of course, once you get into the swing of it, those opening nerves are soon forgotten. But to ensure that you do not tee off to a shakey beginning, from which many people never recover, you have to plan and adopt a positive approach.

Settling down calmly to hit your opening drive will do more than assist in a par at the 1st hole. It will set a pattern for the entire round. I therefore ask that you arrive on the first tee in plenty of time and that you have everything to hand so that when your turn comes to drive, you can move easily into position with a set routine.

In order to develop any movement successfully, it is necessary to break down the movements involved and then rebuild them in your mind. In this way you become familiar with the different sections of the swing, and also with your strengths and weaknesses. Without doubt, this is the best way to move forward.

I want to take you through the golf swing, from address to finish. Basically my programme is structured between flexibility and swing-strengthening exercises. These will build the foundation of the swing and will guard against unnecessary injuries. Half of the professionals on the European PGA Tour endure some pain, and one or two inflict on themselves quite serious damage that will bring a premature end one day to their winning days.

But be warned: all training requires correct preparation. Learning and understanding a movement is one thing; but feeling and enjoying an exercise or a golf swing while performing them is totally different. Only you can teach yourself to feel each move, and casually going through the motions is not enough. Once the correct feeling has been acquired, your game will benefit from the same feel which automatically carries over from one movement to another.

I don't believe that any person can teach another to feel a good golf swing. They can merely point them in the right direction. The feeling must be developed by each individual. Feel is accomplished through focusing on each movement as it takes place.

The brain controls the swing, but the body must be trained to obey. Teaching yourself to feel and understand each movement in golf is crucial. Isolating each exercise as you perform it will develop an understanding about your own strengths and weaknesses and teach you how best to work on each move.

Address to halfway back drill

1 This is the drill: developing the muscle groups to follow a set routine requires discipline and correct repetition. My address position shows a correctly placed right hand. Most club golfers ruin their chances by having their hand too far under the shaft — to cure a slice. It does no such thing; it puts the clubface in a position that makes it unlikely that you will get it back on line, every time. They have to compensate, which as we know, is the kiss of death.
2 This exercise strengthens the load-bearing left hand and arm and side which is essentially the only side that swings the golf club. Note the extention of the left arm, achieved thanks to trunk flexibility and overall left-side

strength. The right elbow remains pointing towards the right hip because I don't want a flying elbow at the top as it might allow the right side to over-dominate the entire swing.

3 To emphasise the total command of the left hand and arm at this point, I am taking my right hand off the club shaft to prepare my special training sequence that can prove of enormous value. If you cannot maintain this position, go down the shaft and shorten the swing.

4 My right hand now remains poised in the position you see, waiting for my left hand to return, with the club. The pause with the left hand must be a brief one when I return to the address position here, because I don't want to break the smooth sequence of this exercise.

2   3   4

Coil for control

Turning against the hips produces torque, or a coil spring effect that should help to drive the ball down the fairway. Some golfers never learn this which means they tend to fan at the ball, rather than hitting it with their fullest power.

I am currently teaching golf writer John Ingham, who assisted me with this book, how he, or any other enthusiastic club player, can grasp this simple, but effective, training method.

So here's how we do it. Taking up your comfortable stance, with your left hand restraining your right hip, make an imaginary backswing with your upper body only. Always ensure that your head is placed just inside your right foot while turning, to guard against falling into a reverse pivot, which is when your head falls towards your left foot at the top of the backswing.

We don't want 'corkscrew' hips rotating wildly. I am demonstrating a proper trunk turn against retaining hips. Now try it yourself.

How to turn the trunk

Boxers talk about hitting their weight to achieve a knock-out punch. In golf we want to do exactly the same thing — knocking the ball straight down the middle. This exercise aims to help you turn the trunk, and develop

ease of movement and co-ordination — essential if you are to bring the clubhead smack into the ball in a consistent way.

Turning the trunk drill

1 Assume a shoulder-width stance and hold your hands away from your chest by about 25cm/10 inches, with your elbows tucked to your sides. Look straight ahead.

2 Turn your trunk as far as possible to your right, ensuring that your hands do not drift apart. Check that your head is 'inside' the right foot.

3 I have turned from right to left, in a sweeping action, transferring my weight so my head is on the 'inside' of the left foot.

Throughout this exercise, make sure that your hands remain at a constant width because if they drift apart, that could enable you to cheat on the full turn.

Rotate that trunk

Without trunk rotation, your golf swing is dead. Doug Sanders' short backswing position was so unusual that it was claimed he could swing in a telephone booth. But believe me, when a short backswing goes wrong, you're in trouble and you need look no further than Sandy Lyle who endured agonies while he re-adjusted his overly short backswing.

This exercise is designed to help those who fail to complete their backswing unless they over-compensate with a swing fault.

Trunk rotation drill

1 Place the ball of your right foot on a golf bag or bench, or whatever, but ensure that the thigh is no higher than horizontal to the ground. Place your left hand just above your knee. Now place your right hand and arm behind your back; get them right behind to create maximum torque and make sure you look straight ahead, and stand erect.

2 Turn your trunk to the maximum back-swing position, while using the left hand to hold back the right leg from moving out of alignment.

Note: the right knee stays facing forwards throughout this trunk rotation exercise while the head remains as it was at the start.

3 Sideways on shows clearly the upper body turn with the lower body held back forcibly by the left hand and arm.

This exercise has an added bonus in that it also develops the left-hand arm and the shoulder and side muscles — the side that is responsible for pulling the clubhead into the ball, from the top of the swing.

> **Caution: Read this again, digest it, and ease your way into this crucial exercise.**

1

2

3

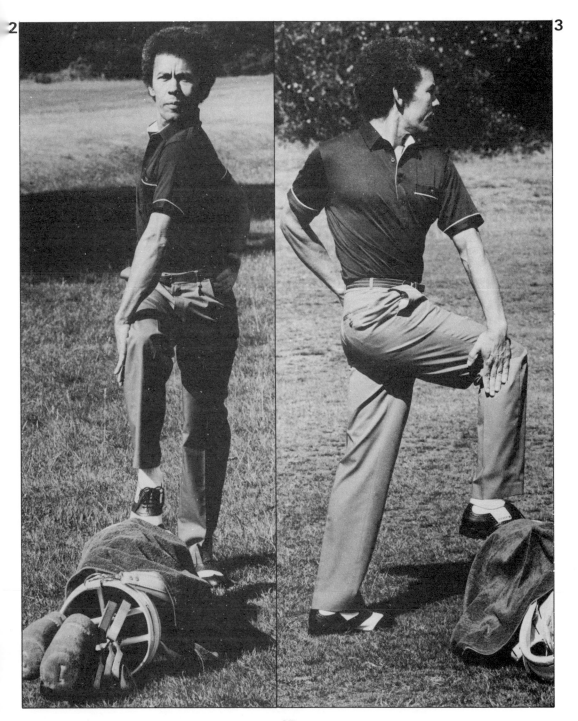

Tone up the abdominal muscles

The exercises shown here help improve your upper body flexibility, which is vital for a good swing.

You can do this seated exercise anywhere and if you don't have a club handy, you can interlock your fingers behind your head and do it while watching TV. It's as simple as that. In fact, it is ideally suited for business-men and office workers waiting for the telephone to ring!

This is a double-barrelled movement be-cause it develops flexibility and slims the mid-section. It emphasises the upper body turn with the minimum hip rotation which, as we've seen, is the key to generating clubhead speed and control.

But it also requires contraction in the abdominal section and that contraction tones those abdominal muscles which, for golfers who over-use the 19th hole, is essential.

Upper body turn drill

1 Sit comfortably and place the club, or a broom, behind your neck. Sit erect — don't slouch.

2 You've no alternative but to turn your upper body while the hips remain constant. Keep looking straight ahead and don't dip your left shoulder.

3 Turning the other way, and this is the follow-through. Again, the hips remain dead ahead and the right shoulder has not dipped.

> Caution: Once again, ease yourself into this exercise if you suffer from upper body inflexibility. You know if your upper body is inflexible if you cannot turn to approximately this position.

1   2   3

Complete upper body flexibility can be enhanced with this neck stretch which requires you to use the natural movement you were born with.

As we grow older we lose our flexibility but a little time and effort can help you to regain the elasticity you had as a child. Although we use our necks every second, lack of full use leads to a tightening in an important area.

Without being able to turn your head, you risk arriving at the top of the swing by turning your whole upper body away from the ball, causing loss of balance and control.

Neck stretch drill
1 Try to look directly over your left shoulder standing to attention.
2 Find the maximum your head can turn with some firm, but gentle, assistance from the left hand. You may hear the occasional grinding sound, but don't worry; this is a highly recommended exercise, particularly for golf.
But remember: Smoothness is essential, looking left and right.

> **Caution: Always turn your shoulder against the head.**

Develop good balance

The European Ryder Cup Captain, Bernard Gallacher, is well aware that balance combined with flexibility is of paramount importance to every golf swing.

At the Apollo Week Volvo Tour Training School at Penina, Portugal, he watched me, along with several other pros, enthusiasts and regular Tour players. He was particularly interested in how to develop balance in some of the pupils.

Several world stars can, in fact, hit full-blooded practice drives while standing on one foot and that is why, when you look at a fine overall swing, the predominant factor is one of rhythm and balance.

Why do I suggest that you stand on one leg as a golfing exercise? The answer is that I want you to become aware that balance is essential.

Balance and flexibility drill

1 Firstly stand on your left leg; cross your right leg over your left with your hands at your sides. Now concentrate on merely balancing in this position for a few seconds and make certain that you are standing ram-rod straight.

Now place the left hand beneath the left thigh, just above the knee as in the picture. Make sure that your right foot is almost alongside the left knee. The right hand is placed with the back of the hand firmly against the back.

2 Turn the shoulders as if on a backswing, using the left hand to pull, corkscrew-fashion, against the right thigh.

This is the perfect exercise to test your balance and flexibility.

Opposite: I am performing the balance and flexibility drill described above under the watchful eye of European Ryder Cup Captain, Bernard Gallacher.

Loosen your trunk

This is a warm-up exercise used by top golfers all over the world. Its benefits, if carried out correctly, are enormous.

The idea here is to loosen the trunk. Many players, however, go wrong by 'dipping' the left shoulder as they turn, thereby putting a strain on the lower right side of the back.

Anyone who practises this exercise should rotate an equal amount of times on both sides for equal body flex on both sides.

Some golfers, such as Bernhard Langer, keep their head behind the shot with such regularity that they increase flexibility in that direction at the expense of flexibility in the opposite direction.

I pointed this out to Bernhard, a winner of the US Masters, and he now realises he has a 'block' when he tries to turn to the left while driving a car. So I suggested that neck turns would help, using the hand-push system. He was so grateful that he wrote me a letter of appreciation.

Neck turns drill

1 Our model stands with her feet apart, as she would when hitting a 4-iron, and her knees are slightly flexed, with the club behind her neck, palms facing forward with head erect.

2 The right leg and foot maintain a consistent line, with the trunk fully turned and, at the same time, she has tried to restrain the hips from over-rotating in order to build up a spring-like position. Repeat to the other side.

> **Caution: Make sure that the head is erect at all times and don't allow the left heel to rise off the ground.**

Building the foundation

The modern golf superstars go jogging and practise stationary cycling. They are not just passing the time of day — they know that strong legs are the foundation of a powerful and athletic game of golf.

On the Ladies Tour, too, the top women golfers take muscle toning seriously. Basically there are not many ways to build strong legs without costly machinery. But here is a good tip which utilizes your own weight to strengthen existing thigh and leg muscle without developing bulk.

Leg strengthening drill

1 Stand with your feet slightly wider than shoulder width apart. Make sure that your toes are turned straight ahead with the legs straight and the knees not bent. Hold the club as shown with the hands wider than shoulder width. Stand with head erect.

2 At all times, keep the arms fully extended as you sweep upwards with your arms to the position illustrated. At the same time, the knees bend in conjunction with the whole motion. As you improve you can increase the 'squat'. Repeat 8 times.

> **Caution: This is also a shoulder stretching exercise. You must not jerk the club upwards but, rather like the ideal swing itself, you should control the smooth movement from start to finish.**

CHAPTER THREE

CHANGE OF DIRECTION

Some parts of the swing are more difficult to develop and control than others. Every individual copes with swing faults in different ways and it has very little to do with the type of golf practice you use to complement your swing.

The body develops the swing that it is capable of reproducing. If the body has good flexibility and co-ordination, the swing you hoped for will have a good chance to develop. In other words, living in the Comfort Zone is what the body does best.

Look at it this way: if you have poor flexibility in the trunk, the only way a correct backswing position can be reached, with the club parallel to the ground, is either by lifting the left heel, or using swing faults, such as collapsing the right knee and ankle, or falling into a reverse pivot.

Arriving at the top of the backswing, in a sound attacking position, is the most effective way to launch the forward swing with total success.

However, think about the right hand and arm position at the top of the backswing. At that point you ought to be able to carry a head-high tray, like some smart restaurant waiters do. From here, starting down on the backswing, and the change of swing direction, are the toughest part of golf. The reason is that the right hand and arm are at a perfect angle to push the club ever upwards, but the weaker left side now has the task of pulling the club the opposite way, into a strong hitting position while, at this split second, the right hand and side must take a temporary break from the action, and not return to it until impact.

However, because most golfers have a strong right side, they tend either to lurch forwards, or hit from the top during the change from swinging back to swinging forwards. Even the experts, when faced with a testing shot, often start the changeover before their backswing is completed, possibly caused by anxiety to get the shot in the air, so you are not alone in this Danger Zone.

With regard to swing speed, let me remind you of gear box changes in a motor car. The almost slow and deliberate gear change, done smoothly at all times, can be likened to the golf swing tempo. The first gear equates to your golf address, to halfway back; second gear takes you nicely to the top of the swing; third gear brings you halfway down; and then you engage top gear for the full flow through the ball.

You would not snatch at a gear change, and you should not rush at a golf swing. The slow, powerful build-up leads to the perfect arrival at the moment of truth — impact. The change in direction from the backswing to the forward swing is the toughest move in golf as Greg Norman can testify. For such an incredibly talented golfer, it seems beyond comprehension that he should admit that he lost, for a while, his way at the top of his swing.

However, it is a position that is filled with danger because you need to keep the swing on track despite lacking a body capable of windmill sail precision.

Swing drill

1 What you need here is trunk rotation, balance and poise because without these the

body might warp towards various swing faults.

The reason I have my hands in this split-grip is to allow the left hand and arm to pull against the resisting right hand and arm. It develops the pulling muscles in the left shoulder and the left-hand side muscles.

My right leg is bent to resist the hips over-rotating and notice the importance of the right leg as the chief load-bearer. There is almost no weight on the left leg at this key point.

2 The 'pulling the chain' effect and the left side can be developed much more efficiently with this split hand system. The reason is that the right hand is pulling against the left, thus preventing a 'casting' action. This also serves as an excellent wrist stretch exercise

for those with inflexible wrists. Notice how the hips are now square to the target, which means that I have rotated square to the target-line.

3 This is the moment of truth in any golf swing and the end of this particular Swing Drill. Up to this point the right hand has continued to resist the pulling action of the left. The right hand, in fact, is actually helping to prevent the left hand from uncocking too soon.

Note that the rotation of the hips has continued naturally and this is the moment when the right hand and side should take control to deliver the 'hit' to the swing which has been guided, up until now, predominantly by the left hand, arm and side.

Obviously I am not recommending that you split your hands on the shaft while playing a round of golf. This is merely an exercise routine. However, some golfers use the baseball, or two-handed, grip, with all the fingers on the shaft, and they claim that this gives them extra control in retaining the angle of the downswing.

Caution: Do not jerk at any time during the performance of this exercise movement. It should be one continuous pulling action.

Opposite: Ted's golf swing. By exercising regularly to maximize his personal fitness, strength and flexibility he has improved his swing and thereby his whole game. Note that the rotation of the hips has continued naturally.

3

Build up your left side

Because golf and the downswing are controlled almost entirely by the left hand, arm and side from the top of the swing to the horizontal position, it makes sense to develop this vital side of the body, assuming that you are a right-handed golfer.

The stronger muscle groups always control any movement and they are dominant. And if the stronger side of a weekend golfer is the right-hand side (as is the case in most right-handed people), the tendency for them is to try to 'kill' the ball by hitting the daylights out of it with the right side. However, this is the opposite of what we are striving for.

The solution, therefore, is to over-ride this natural urge by building up a massively strong left side. In my view it is impossible to have a left hand and arm that are too strong.

In the following exercises we outline the number of sets and repetitions that will deal with this power-building area. But it is interesting to see in these photographs that even though our model has 'choked' down the shaft to make the weight less severe, she still found difficulty in controlling the club, while she curved away in order to reduce the strain on an arm that would benefit from this very exercise.

Left-side power building drill
1 Stand with feet shoulder width apart and your right arm behind your back. Hold the club in your left hand with the clubhead raised at shoulder height.
2 This is the end of the drill with the arm and body in a better position and you can see that the strain has been eased with the elbows straighter. Lower the club slowly to a horizontal position. Hold for a count of 2 or 3 seconds and repeat 8 times.

3 John Ingham demonstrates the 'quit' on the training drill brought about by lack of strength in the hands, wrists and forearms. The cure for all of this is to stop at the horizontal position on every repetition.

The difference between the professional and the club player lies largely in this area. Obviously the professional hits thousands more shots than does the amateur and therefore builds up the retain-and-release muscles.

Any amateur can develop flexible wrists, strong hands and forearms by repeating this drill, together with other specific drills in this book.

Develop left arm power

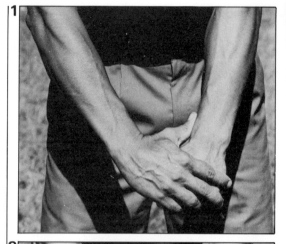

Since we have established that the left hand and arm must dictate proceedings up until the split second when we change direction, it is essential that the left arm must be powerful. However, a flexible left wrist is a colossal bonus because it guards against injury.

To develop the left arm's power and flexibility so that it can fully control and override the usually dominant right side, I am now going to tell you how to take a short-cut to the kind of power that the professionals have developed through hitting millions of practice shots.

Left arm power drill

1 My left arm is hanging straight down, just on the inside of my left leg — the hitting position. Use the right hand to grip the left, as illustrated. Particularly note the position of the right-hand thumb.

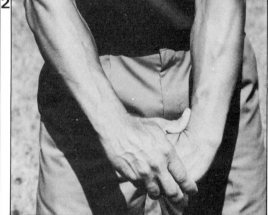

2 Make sure that the left arm is extended and the left fist is 'flat' to the wrist, and clenched. Gently pull the right hand back against the left; the pressure of the right thumb helps create maximum left wrist stretch. This exercise can be done anytime anywhere and you should reverse it and practise with the other hand for added power balance.

3 This photo shows what happens to a blocked and inflexible wrist. Also, the left arm is in need of development which can be achieved through our specific drills regarding one-handed swing routines.

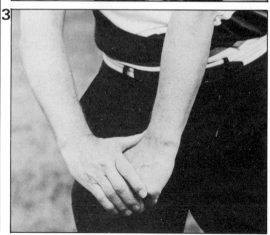

> Caution: Don't jerk the wrist back; rather use consistent pressure. You should continue practising this exercise routine over a period of seven months to a year.

Build a strong left wrist

If your left wrist breaks down during the downswing, there is no way of hitting a solid golf shot. These photographs show how to build up a strong left wrist, which is not liable to collapse because of incorrect training.

Left wrist power drill

1 This shows the preparation with an up-and-down movement we call a reverse wrist curl. This requires a 'contest' between your two hands to build up a strong, firm left wrist. The technique requires a constant resistance of the right hand against the up-and-down movement of the left wrist.

2 Think of a see-saw movement of the left wrist, climbing up and down, despite the constant resistance of your right hand. Do not let the left wrist collapse on the downward movement — and feel the strain in the left forearm.

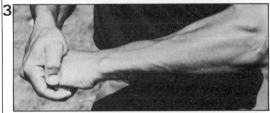

3 This demonstrates that we always return to the position shown in photograph 1 which is matching the impact position where the greatest strain — near impact — is imposed on the left wrist.

4 Pulling back the wrist encourages this position at impact — which we don't want. Make sure that you avoid this.

5 Many pros have been squeezing a squash ball for years, but doing it wrongly. When they squeeze they should resist the urge to curl the wrist upwards. The 'flat' squeeze position is where the four muscle groups are at their weakest and in need of the correct boost.

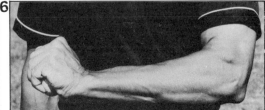

6 In this picture, the grip is at its strongest, and from our point of view, this angle creates untold problems — for golfers. This exercise should be carried out on *both* hands.

You, too, can have a swing like Snead's

One of the greatest golfing swings the world has ever seen is that used for years by Sam Snead from Virginia in the United States. The way he hit the ball and his rhythm were always a lesson in itself.

However well golfers may swing the club, the impact position must always be similar if they are to dispatch the ball down the fairway to its intended target. Obviously there are a few great professional golfers whose swings withstand comparison with that of Snead, but I have studied Snead's swing in particular and, like most other golfers, would love to emulate it. This is what I have tried to do as you will see from studying the photographs of our respective swings. By doing so, you may also pick up some vital ingredients that you can incorporate within your own golf.

Building that arm

This exercise requires the strength that you must develop in order to achieve your potential power in the vital hitting area. This drill will test your ability and will tell you if your hands and arms can cope with the part of the swing that matters most.

While the exercise looks self-explanatory, you must guard against dropping your arm below the horizontal because this means that you have 'wilted' and will not gain anything from the disciplined exercise.

Weaker golfers attempting this exercise may feel inclined to put their hands further down the grip or bend their elbow slightly. This is understandable but as development takes place, their arm extension will happen naturally, as they build up power.

Arm building drill
1 Hold the club vertically in your left hand with your arm fully extended. Make certain that the left wrist remains 'flat' and does not collapse.
2 Rotate the club to your right, using a slow controlled movement. At no time must the clubhead dip below the horizontal position.
3 Rotate back to the other side, maintaining a flat wrist in a slow, firm sweep. Keep your right hand behind your back throughout this exercise as it promotes the thought of keeping the right side out of the golf shot until absolutely necessary.

> **Caution: If you feel a burning sensation, pause and resume the exercise later.**

Controlling the turn

I have trained at karate and that particular martial arts skill requires perfect hip and hand co-ordination in order to deliver a maximum blow with controlled power. Hand speed without hip rotation will not work powerfully with a golf swing. I have experienced both sports and know that certain movements and body co-ordination in golf and karate are common, and this could be beneficial to the golfer.

Many club golfers merely swing at the ball because they lack position and balance and, without balance, nothing works in golf — or karate. While I advocate that the upper body turns against restraining hips during the backswing, the power comes from timing the release of the entire body at the moment of impact, rather like a flash of lightning as it strikes. This means that you must maximize your energy potential. Sadly, many golfers fail to grasp this and soldier on for years not making any attempt to *learn to hit their weight.*

Controlling the hips drill

1 This position shown by John Ingham is halfway back. He is attempting to turn his trunk while not over-turning his hips as he believed that one of his faults was over-rotating hips.

2 However, in this picture I have guided him towards a more controlled hip movement, which is more suitable for a top backswing position. After working on this exercise, John found that better balance and control were within his capabilities.

3 The secret of the exercise is to generate hip thrust as used in some types of karate training. But many golfers fear to do this because they have injured their backs, due to the body's lack of ability to control the swing without getting into compensating

positions — something many good players do without realising their mistake.

4 In this position John has turned to the left and his head is in alignment with his left foot but his weight remains too much on his right side. And notice, too, the incomplete turn of the hips causing his weight to stay on the ball of the right foot.

5 What we strive for, in fact, is illustrated by me: complete hip turn, head directly above the inside of my left foot, and my belt buckle facing slightly left of the target. No weight remains on the right foot; in fact, I could easily lift that foot. Gary Player often walks through the shot at this very point. By the way, Gary Player and Ted Pollard make quite a double act in a demonstration of this walk through the hit, and we once did it to great amusement on the Northwestern Exhibition Stand at St Andrews!

Towards the finish

What has taken place at impact is revealed if you study the movement from the impact position through to the finish. In many cases this is a complete give-away to a professional's trained eye who is looking for ways to improve a pupil. This is proof that videos and still pictures are an essential aid to good golf teaching.

1 For instance, if you look at this picture you might gain the impression that an effective shot has been struck. Not so. Unhappily the head of our student has turned to follow the flight of the ball while her weight has remained too much on her right side. This action is the result of hitting 'too early' and this has forced the hands to get ahead of the body. Because of the early hit, her hands can no longer rotate with power and control through the impact zone.

2 What we should strive for is the position shown here where my head is still looking at where the ball was resting. My weight is now almost entirely on my left side and my hands have rotated with *maximum* force through the shot.

3 At the finish of this particular shot, our pupil reveals her higher level of playing skill with a beautiful, well-balanced, finish.

Opposite: Frank Nobilo of New Zealand is one of the most promising young players in the world today. However, this finish is not as upright as it should be and could lead to back strain.

CHAPTER FOUR

COMMON SWING FAULTS

To see yourself as others see you is very hard and looking in a mirror as you hit a golf ball could prove inconvenient, if not impossible!

One of the major faults that afflicts the average weekend player is what we call the reverse pivot. Simply put, this is when a player almost falls over backwards at the top of the backswing.

The reverse pivot (opposite)
If we were to draw a white line from the inside of our pupil's right heel upwards, we would find that her head is several inches too far towards the target. Where it should be, however, is slightly further back, just inside an imaginary line to inside her right heel.

Hitting from the top (below)
In this picture, our student demonstrates another awful fault — hitting from the top. It is essential to control the change of direction from the backswing to the downswing. In many cases golfers hit viciously from the top of their backswing, which is like a fisherman casting his line.

However, in the case of the golfer, the power has been spent too soon. What we need is to store that power until the opportune moment arrives.

1

Reverse pivot and collapsed right foot

1 The address position for this slightly downhill shot would seem, on the face of it, to be acceptable, despite a slight over-crouch. However, what happens next is sheer disaster even though, according to John Ingham, this was a posed shot. This is quite a common fault experienced by many weekend golfers and high handicappers.

2 The problem here is caused by lack of trunk flexibility and therefore the body compensates, either by this collapse of the right foot and knee, or by falling into what we call a reverse pivot. Some gifted players can take liberties and try to groove their swing faults to their body ability but very seldom do these players succeed or indeed stay at the top. This problem usually starts about halfway into the backswing, and once an error is initiated, there is no way to correct it satisfactorily.

3 Here is John at the top of the backswing. This deliberate position exactly mirrors many swings that you see on golf courses throughout the world, and many professional coaches opt for the easy way out by recommending a shorter backswing. However, the best remedy is trunk flexibility and developing strong legs — there is no other way.

4 Here I am at the top of the backswing, demonstrating the action and body position that you should strive for. Note the position of my right foot and knee.

2

3

4

1

Flying elbow

1 The right elbow of most club golfers does not know what it is doing. It behaves badly as shown in this picture of me at the top of the swing. What happens is that the inner rotation of the right arm and shoulder is not capable of holding the correct position at the top of the backswing. So how do we work towards a lasting cure?

2 Firstly look at the correct top of the swing position illustrated here. Notice how the right elbow is pointing directly towards the right hip, not giving it any opportunity to wander. In this way the left hand and arm can remain in complete control whereas in picture **1** the right hand and arm, with a contraction of the right shoulder muscles, would seem set upon making an early attacking move — which we don't want.

3 To remedy this swing fault, just follow the exercise shown here. Place your hand directly in front of your right shoulder with the palm of the hand facing *downwards*. Now then, keep the right arm extended like mine and rotate round to the left with the shoulders remaining totally square, unlike John (left). This is a repetition exercise, to be repeated 8 to 12 times with both hands. However, do not exceed this in any one session.

Caution: Repeat no more than three sets at any one session. And make sure that your arm is extended fully at all times.

CHAPTER FIVE

TIPS FROM THE TOP

No top professional golfer is so good that he does not feel the need to listen to sound advice. At the PGA European Tour School I create Fitness Programmes for all the players. Everyone is keen to pick up ideas and learn, even at the highest level where professionals experiment with different shafts, grip thicknesses and techniques which help create more positive thinking. With this in mind, Alan Fine has provided his own approach on how a golfer should think as he tees up for a round that could change his life and professional future.

In Spain and Portugal I took time out to work with Anders Sorenson of Denmark, V.J. Singh of Fiji, and Bernard Gallacher who is still seeking to improve even though he is now no longer on the full circuit.

One of the top tips I learnt from these

Below: Here in Portugal I worked with some of the top professionals on the European Tour to improve their levels of overall fitness.

professionals is illustrated above. My student is warming up the shoulder areas which will guard against any injuries in the shoulder region. Many golf players find this a vulnerable part and tend not to fully extend through the shot because of discomfort.

Shoulder warm-up drill

1 To do this exercise extend your right arm fully, and clasp the back of the right elbow with your left hand, as shown. Notice that the right arm is out of alignment with the body here.

2 Pull the outstretched right arm the opposite way to create flexibility in the shoulders which will assist in a better top of the backswing position and guard against that flying right elbow.

> **Caution: Be careful not to force the arms across because this will create unwanted pain. Also, the further back the right arm can go behind your head, the more benefit you will receive. And, as with all these exercises, you should work with both sides and arms to keep the body in balance.**

Here's to added power

Power comes from a combination of strength, balance flexibility and co-ordination. But without correct stance and alignment, you will blast away with a hit-or miss game. To help develop this, try practising the training drill shown here.

One-armed training drill

1 This training drill requires enormous left hand, arm and side strength and flexibility. Notice that I deliberately place my right hand firmly against my rump to keep that right side as 'quiet' as possible throughout the swing. But my trunk has turned while maintaining an extended left arm. This puts me in the power position.

2 Here is my pupil performing the same exercise — perfectly.

Body check

To help you line up correctly, dead on target, follow this tried and tested routine and only allow the professional to check you out.

This body alignment check has often been an eye-opener to certain well-known professionals who had not realised they were aiming off-centre.

Golfing fundamentals

However hard you have tried and however much you have achieved at improving your strength and all-round flexibility, you also need to take a look at the basic fundamentals of golf. Here Hugh Boyle illustrates this for us.

1 A relaxed address position, with no obvious crouching or visible tension, should always be in your script.

2 To demonstrate how many professionals train to maintain a repeating grip, Hugh

emphasises the importance of where the left hand should be placed.

3 & 4 Hugh also shows the most popular overlap grip (left) and the interlocking grip (above) used by Jack Nicklaus and some other professionals. Some experts favour the two-handed 'baseball' grip but often, when teaching others, advocate the Harry Vardon overlap grip.

Always remember, whatever else you do, that grip and alignment need to be checked and re-checked. Make a habit of getting it right and you will reap rich dividends.

CHAPTER SIX

ALL YOU NEED TO KNOW

about clubs, balls and shafts

If you want to get the very best out of your individual game, whether your're a professional or a club golfer, you need to know which equipment suits you.

It is no use playing with the clubs Nick Faldo uses, unless those clubs are fitted with a shaft compatible with your strength and swing tempo.

Many sales people try to sell the products they have in stock, rather than tailor a club selection to suit an individual. And many will try to sell you a set of clubs even though they have never seen you swing at a ball.

However, a caring professional, and there are many of them, is your best guide provided that you have some basic facts from which to work. He can help.you form a clear idea of your own needs.

The trouble is that few weekend golfers really understand exactly which equipment would best suit them. So here is a clear explanation of all you need to know about clubs, balls and probably the most overlooked aspect — the shafts.

The following information has been put together in collaboration with experts in the business and I'd like to take this opportunity to thank them.

Which club?

Persimmon woods
Traditional wood is the material used in the best clubs for good looks and exceptional feel. Appreciated by low-handicap amateurs and pros who can work the ball from tee to

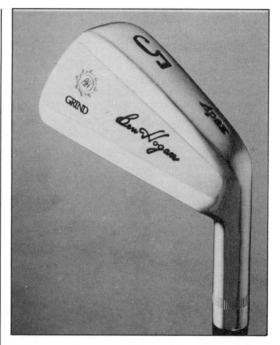

This apex iron was deisgned by Ben Hogan.

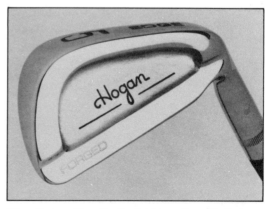

The first cavity-backed 'forged' golf club.

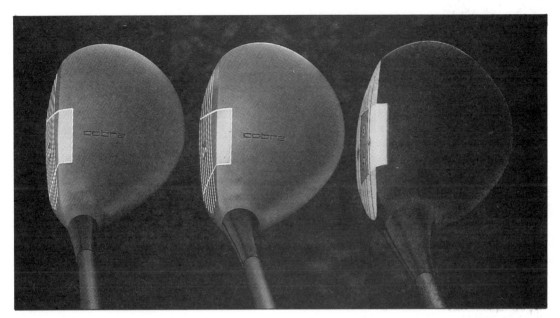

These metal and persimmon woods are popular with pros and low-handicappers.

green, they are available in a variety of attractive finishes and face insert options.

Metalwoods

Very popular with all golfers, these investment cast woods are foam filled and offer a low centre of gravity and perimeter weighting to help golfers obtain higher ball trajectory and straighter hits.

Blade irons

Traditional irons forged from carbon steel are popular with low-handicap amateurs and those pros who appreciate their feel and control which can contribute to good striking. Chrome or satin finish provide that classic look.

Cavity back irons

Cast from stainless steel, these heads have become popular and can help the average golfer to hit the ball better. Large heads combined with heel and toe weighting and progressive offset make shotmaking easier. A new development is soft-feel perimeter weighted clubs with a blade face cast from high-alloy carbon steel.

This selection of 5 irons shows a regular iron, a baffler, a ladies' and a super senior iron.

Which shaft?

It is important that the clubs you use have the right shaft characteristics so that the clubhead will be in the correct position at impact to deliver the maximum desired shot. As much as 70 per cent of a shot emanates from the shaft so it is important to choose the right one.

The 'feel' of the club is defined by how much the shaft bends during the swing, and if you are a discerning golfer, you will soon notice whether the flex is right or wrong. The right one for you is that which best suits your swing speed and timing and thereby assists you in achieving maximum accuracy and distance.

If you are very strong with a positive hand action, then you can probably use standard weight shafts with confidence. However, high handicappers and less physically strong golfers would be better advised to use lightweight shafts to generate more club head speed and thereby achieve greater distance.

Although shafts can have the same flex, they may have different kick-points. Low-handicap players usually prefer a high kick-point with more flexibility in the butt end, whereas average players need a low kick-point to help them get the ball airborne.

Which golf ball is best for you?

There are dozens of different makes of golf ball and when you consider that there are 40 million golfers world-wide, each owning not less than a dozen balls each, you know that this world is heavily populated with these works of art. The modern ball may seem expensive but it is a high-class product, whichever manufacturer produced it. And one of those 'fly miles' illegal missiles sold in the United States and Japan is mind-blowing.

The average golfer is usually better off with a solid no-cut ball, whereas the better player who wants to use controlled spin on the ball opts for the balata rubber wound ball. Rapid development of golf ball technology has been a major influence on the growth of the game. Today's golf balls are high-tech products and golfers have never had a wider choice.

There are four major types of ball available today whose differing constructions result in widely differing playing characteristics. Thus players of all abilities are able to find a ball best suited to their play. However, all of them represent a quantum leap in manufacturing technology since the early days of golf back in fifteenth-century Holland when they were made from boxwood or stuffed leather.

The Haskell ball, which arrived early this century, is the forerunner of the modern three-piece ball. It had a gutta-percha core wrapped with yards of rubber thread, onto which was moulded a gutta-percha cover. The Haskell popularized golf with its superior performance — greater distance and control — and also introduced dimple patterns.

Another development was the replacement of solid centres by liquid centres, which held sway until the 1970s when one-piece and two-piece balls of great durability were perfected. In this decade, manufacturers committed more resources to dimple pattern research as a means of improving ball performance within the parameters established by golf's governing bodies.

The DDH (dodecahedron) pattern balls use dimples of three different sizes arranged in pentagonal groups. These balls are considered to be the most symmetrical — and hence aerodynamic — pattern available. This provides the player at every level with balls that perform to the highest degree of distance, accuracy and control.

Modern golf balls with their Surlyn covers do not cut when mishit as was the case up to a few years ago with balata balls. This makes them better value for money and adds to your enjoyment of the game. However, for professionals and accomplished amateurs, balata balls are still widely available as they offer an additional degree of control by having a slightly softer cover. This enables good players to impart more spin on the ball to give greater control, especially on short shots near the green.

The four types of modern golf ball are:

One-piece ball
This is the simplest type of ball to manufacture and the least effective in performance. Compression moulded from a plug of rubber, it is inexpensive and often used on driving ranges.

Two-piece ball
This has an inner core of about 3.75cm/1.5inches in diameter made from a resilient material, and a compression moulded cover or shell. Injection moulding is being increasingly used to form the cover with greater precision and so give even better performance from what is an extremely effective type of golf ball. Two-piece balls are hard, long lasting and give distance, but this hardness can make them too 'lively' for chipping and putting. However, most golfers value the extra distance and durability they give above a marginal loss of control on short shots.

Three-piece (or thread-wound) ball
The small rubber sphere is surrounded by tightly wound elastic thread to give high compression and resilience and then given a tough Surlyn cover, similar to that on a

An aerodynamic DDH patterned ball.

two-piece ball. The three-piece ball gives slightly less distance than a two-piece but it does offer greater control by accepting more backspin.

The balata ball
The construction is similar to that of a thread-wound ball except that the centre is usually a hollow rubber sphere filled with clay paste and water. The centre is frozen before being wrapped in elastic thread. The cover is processed natural balata which has been vulcanized.

The balata cover is very soft compared with Surlyn, and its liquid centre gives optimum feel and control. Professionals invariably use balata balls since a slight loss of distance is irrelevant compared with the capability it gives them to 'shape' their shots and exercise a high degree of control. However, the disadvantage of these balls is that they are easily damaged by mishits. They are also expensive and therefore little used by the average amateur.

CHAPTER SEVEN

COMPUTERS

The Japanese are into golf in a huge way and, as everyone knows, are both brilliant creators and inventors. Their latest input is a portable computer that comes to the aid of the golf professional.

This incredible mechanical 'brain' is placed on the floor or turf in front of a golf driving net and the golf balls are teed up on a rubber tee or from a simulated 'fairway', on a rubberized surface.

When the shot is hit (and in the pictures we see Simon Buckley, the pro at Ham Manor, West Sussex, in action), the computer automatically registers clubhead speed, the exact distance the shot would carry and whether the clubface was square, open or shut.

The only thing this little wizard cannot do is to offer you advice and that must come, as before, from a professional.

Why do I recommend this new golfing innovation? For starters, any machine that tells you about your own clubhead speed obviously knows its business. How will it help to know *your* own clubhead speed? I know that certain experts swing a driver at an average speed of approximately 115mph and if their clubhead is square at that speed they should hit a reasonable shot!

I believe that Ian Woosnam hits at an even faster speed, but he has exceptional hand and arm co-ordination through the impact zone.

Knowing your own clubhead speed, when swinging smoothly could help you by preventing unwanted lashing of the ball, which produces negative results.

At present, this computer is only on sale in Japan but I feel sure that it will not be long before it makes its appearance in Europe and the United States. It will make a considerable impact on the teaching of the game in enclosed spaces.

Computer courtesy of Matsushita Electric Works Company, Osaka, Japan

Index

Numerals in *italics* refer to illustrations